6-3-98 Retirement Party
Lindee & Joe

Joan Winmill Brown

The Shelter

OF

His Wings

A BOOK OF HOPE
AND COMFORT

Illustrations by Frank Riccio

The C.R.Gibson Company, Norwalk, Connecticut 06856

INTRODUCTION

One night in California, during a violent storm, I looked out my window, and spotted beneath a hedge, a picture of absolute peace. In spite of gale winds that were bending seemingly indomitable trees, and flashes of lightning illuminating the sky and heralding deafening thunder—there was a mother bird with her wings outstretched, sheltering her contented, sleeping baby.

It was a moment that brought back the words from Psalms 61: 4 from the Living Bible "…Oh, to be safe beneath the shelter of Your wings!" Personal storms often come into our lives—unannounced, uninvited. We are confronted with devastating changes that rock the security we have taken for granted. They come in many forms— through severe illness, bereavement, a loved one who has caused great heartache, etc. For such times our Lord has promised to be with us, giving strength and comfort for all our needs. We can know the shelter of His wings and live in peace and security.

As I wrote this book, I included many writings and Scriptures that I have collected over the years. They have consoled me in the past and continue to bring me hope. May you, too, find in them our Lord's encouragement and solace, as you live each day with Him.

Wings of Love

How precious is Your lovingkindness, O God!
Therefore the children of men
put their trust under the shadow
of Your wings.

PSALMS 36:7

*A*ll of us need to know that we are loved. Love from others can turn our darkest moments into ones of joy. To know that we are loved by our Creator, however, brings a joy that will last forever.

One definition of the word "shadow" is: an inseparable companion. To think that God is our inseparable companion, protecting us beneath the "shadow of His wings," enables us to soar above all the heartaches, the pain, the everyday stress that confronts us. We are not alone. We are loved.

God is the presence, warm, all-enfolding,
touching the drab world into brilliance,
lifting the sad heart into song,
indescribable, beyond understanding,
yet by a bird's note, a chord of music,
a light at sunset, a sudden movement of rapt insight,
a touch of love, making the whole universe
a safe home for the soul.

AN EARLY CHRISTIAN

*B*irds teach me so much about the love of God. Their resiliency is amazing. After a great storm in which the winds buffeted our house until I thought the roof would be ripped off, and the rain was coming down in thunderous sheets, I kept wondering how birds that nest in our hedges were faring. I suggested to my husband Bill, that perhaps we should get a tarpaulin and put it over the hedges, but he said emphatically, "No, that's God's work! He'll take care of them." I was still concerned. However, the next morning I looked out my kitchen window and there were the birds lined up, as usual, waiting for me to feed them. They were as spunky as ever. In fact, a lark overhead was singing its melodious song and several other birds were in the birdbath, carrying out their morning ablutions! God had certainly taken care of them, and once more I was amazed by His lovingkindness and my lack of faith for the wellbeing of His creatures.

And the God of love and peace will be with you.
II CORINTHIANS 13:11

*D*uring the Civil War in America, a truce was called and the opposing armies stared bitterly at each other across a war-scarred field. Many of the men were in dire conditions. Hungry and wounded, their morale was at an all time low. From out of the field flew a small, brown bird. Up it soared and when it was only a dot in the sky, the men heard it singing. It was a skylark and its glorious song brought gladness to the hearts of those soldiers. Their anger and bitterness were exchanged for tears and hope. They were reminded that God still cared for them.

Dear God,

let me soar in the face of the wind;
up—
up—
like the lark,

so poised and so sure,
through the cold
in the storm
with wings to endure.

let the silver rain wash
all the dust from my wings,
let me soar
as he soars,

let me sing
as he sings;
let it lift me
all joyous
and carefree
and swift,

let it buffet
and drive me
but, God,
let it lift.

RUTH BELL GRAHAM

*A*nyone who met Corrie ten Boom could not help being amazed by her radiance. Even when she was in her eighties, there was still that same dynamic resolve that had once brought this Dutch woman through the horrors of a Nazi concentration camp. She believed totally in God's unfailing love and continued to experience it in that most unlikely of places.

Corrie told me:

"When I was taken to Ravensbruck everything in my life had fallen. At roll call with 96,000 other inmates, we had to stand for hours in the bitter cold. The guards would beat the prisoners and I could hardly bear to see it and hear their cries. One morning, as dawn was breaking, a bird began to sing. We looked up in the sky and saw a skylark singing its heart out. I was instantly reminded of Psalms 103:11:

> *For as the heavens are high above the earth,*
> *So great is His mercy toward those who fear Him.*

For three weeks God sent that skylark to sing through that dreaded roll call. It kept my eyes turned in the right direction."

When she was so ill towards the end of her life, she could hardly speak. Yet she would point heavenward and whisper, "Jesus," her eyes still radiant.

One of her favorite sayings was, "There is no pit deep enough that God's love is not there." When I experience tragedies that seem ready to break me, I remember those words of hers and I am reminded that nothing can separate us from God's unfailing love.

For I am persuaded that neither death nor life, nor
angels nor principalities nor powers, nor things present,
nor things to come, nor height nor depth, nor any other
created thing, shall be able to separate us from the love
of God, which is in Christ Jesus, our Lord.

ROMANS 8:38-39

*I*n my travels around the world I have enjoyed collecting
small boxes. It started because they were easy and light to
pack, but my collection grew because of their beauty and
endless variety. Family and friends saw that I collected them and
gradually gave me exquisite pieces. I keep them on a small table
in my bedroom and their craftsmanship, color, and beauty continually remind me of countries visited and those who are dear
to me.

Several years ago, I was given a small pink alabaster box by
some missionaries in Italy. Each time I see it, I think of them and
pray for their ministry. It is a special box, for I am
reminded of it by Mary of Bethany who came to
Jesus with the most precious possession she had—
an alabaster box filled with spikenard ointment.
In those days, the price of that spikenard would
have cost her almost a year's wages. It was with
great sacrifice she came that night with her gift
for Jesus.

As she poured the precious ointment over
Jesus' head, Mary was criticized by those who had
gathered in the house of Simon. She was the only
one of His followers who seemed to understand

the announcements he had made concerning His pending death and resurrection. This was her gift to Him to symbolize the preparation of His body for burial.

My alabaster box is empty. I keep it that way as a reminder of what I would like to be able to fill it with for our Lord, for all of His love and sacrifice. I cannot give Him ointment, but symbolically, I can fill it with promises of my time—time to tell others about His great love for them and time to help someone in His name. One gift I could give would be more time spent in prayer with Him, for most of all, He desires my whole life and my whole heart, surrendered completely to Him.

Today, wherever we are, we can surrender our lives and give our Lord the gift of our love.

> *Were the whole realm of nature mine,*
> *That were an offering far too small;*
> *Love so amazing, so divine,*
> *Demands my soul, my life, my all.*
>
> ISAAC WATTS

Be generous in your surrender! Meet His measureless devotion for you with a measureless devotion to Him. Be glad and eager to hand over the control of your life to Him. Whatever there is of you, let Him have it all. Give up forever everything that separates you from Him.

HANNAH WHITALL SMITH
(PARAPHRASED BY CATHERINE JACKSON)

After an air raid in London, England, during World War II, a young boy who had been severely wounded was brought to the hospital. Little hope was given for his recovery. When he was finally identified, his mother was contacted and told to come to him as quickly as possible.

She arrived to find him unconscious. Her beloved child lay motionless in a stark hospital bed. The doctors told her not to touch him or talk to him, as any excitement might cause him to die. "He will not know you, anyway," they cautioned. "It is best that you wait outside." After she pleaded with them to let her at least sit by him, they finally agreed to her grief stricken request.

For hours she sat by her young son, as doctors and nurses came and went checking on his condition. Later, while totally exhausted and forgetting her promise not to touch or speak to him, she instinctively leaned forward and gently stroked his forehead. Suddenly, with his eyes still closed, a hint of a smile appeared on the boy's face. "Mother, you are here," he whispered. Instantly, he had recognized the loving touch of his mother and it was the turning point to his recovery.

It is Jesus' loving touch when we are ill, or in dire need of help, that can bring us peace. He is our constant companion.

> *Speak to Him, thou, for He hears, and Spirit*
> *with Spirit can meet—*
> *Closer is He than breathing,*
> *and nearer than hands and feet.*
> ALFRED, LORD TENNYSON

Stone walls do not a prison make,
Nor iron bars a cage;
Minds innocent and quiet take
That for an hermitage;
If I have freedom in my love
And in my soul am free,
Angels alone, that soar above,
Enjoy such liberty.

RICHARD LOVELACE

Amidst the horror of a Nazi prison, the brilliant theologian and Christian minister Dietrich Bonhoeffer never faltered in his belief in the love of God. Because of his courageous stand against Hitler, he was imprisoned for most of the war years and executed in 1945. It was only a few days later that the prison camp in which he died was liberated by the Allies.

The Nazis thought they could silence Bonhoeffer and his influence, but his writings live on to enrich us spiritually. They help to encourage us through hardships, knowing that the same Lord is with us, who gave Bonhoeffer strength to face his trials. God was his, and is our inseparable companion.

Lord, whatever this day may bring,
Thy name be praised. . .
O God be gracious unto me and help me.
Give me the strength to bear
    what Thou dost send,
    and do not let fear rule over me. . .
I trust in thy grace,
    and commit my life wholly into Thy hands.
Do with me according to Thy will
    and as is best for me.
Whether I live or die, I am with Thee,
    and Thou, my God, art with me,
Lord, I wait for Thy salvation
    and for Thy kingdom.

DIETRICH BONHOEFFER

*W*e may never have to face the bitter experience of prison, but nevertheless we can heed the example of those who have come before us and gather courage to face our own days of heartache and fear. We must remember that we, too, share the same grace and love of God each moment of every day.

I used to feel as if I were in a prison. Oh, the bars were invisible, but nevertheless I felt a prisoner—a prisoner within my mind and soul. We make our own prisons when we shut out God.

But Christ can give thee heart who loveth thee:
Can set thee in the eternal ecstasy
Of his great jubilee:
Can give thee dancing heart and
shining face,
And lips filled full of grace,
And pleasure of the rivers and the sea.
Who knocketh at his door
He welcomes evermore.

CHRISTINA ROSSETTI

*S*leep evaded me that night. Sleeping in a strange bed, miles from home, I missed the familiar surroundings of my own bedroom. At five a.m. I started to drift off to sleep—only to be awakened by the sound of a cuckoo.

"Oh, please don't start," I thought, "all the rest of the birds will begin singing. It will be a full dawn chorus." My fears became reality. One by one, the birds began to sing and soon the whole valley resonated with their voices. Sleep was now out of the question. Feeling rather annoyed at their intrusive singing, I staggered out of bed to watch the dawn.

The sun's rays were just beginning to filter through the trees, standing like sentinels on the surrounding hills that were covered in a light gossamer mist. The sight was sheer beauty and my momentary irritation vanished, as I became a spectator to God's magnificent artistry.

Now the bird's dawn chorus took on new meaning for me. It became a hymn of praise—a glorious cantata to rival even the great Johann Sebastian Bach or George Frederick Handel. I felt

moved to join this winged chorus in a prayer of thanksgiving to God for His loving care for us. The trees that housed the choristers swayed gently in the wind and the scene became imprinted on my mind.

I now welcome the memory of that cuckoo who awakened the chorus and disturbed my sleep. On dark days, I remember the song of those birds who, even before they started out on their daily search for food, sang with such joy. I, too, am reminded that "In all things give thanks unto the Lord..." and the wonder of His Love for each one of us.

> *O, Lord, that lends me life*
> *Lend me a heart replete with thankfulness.*
> WILLIAM SHAKESPEARE

> *Oh, give thanks to the Lord,*
> *for He is good:*
> *For His mercy endures forever.*
> *Oh, that men would give thanks to the Lord*
> *for His goodness,*
> *And for His wonderful works*
> *to the children of men!*
> *For He satisfies the longing soul,*
> *And fills the hungry soul with goodness.*
> *Let them sacrifice the sacrifices of thanks-*
> *giving, And declare His works*
> *with rejoicing.*
> PSALMS 107:1,8-9,22

Wings of Peace

If I take the wings of the morning,
And dwell in the uttermost parts of the sea,
Even there Your hand shall lead me,
And Your right hand shall hold me.

PSALMS 139:9-10

Strong Son of God, immortal Love,
Whom we, that have not seen thy face,
By faith, and faith alone, embrace,
Believing where we cannot prove.

ALFRED, LORD TENNYSON

*W*hen we travel abroad, strange customs and different cultures can make us feel alone. However, a simple familiar sight can help us remember that God is always there. One such sight is that of the tiny sparrow. In China or India, you may find slight variations in their markings, but the same cheeky little bird is found almost everywhere.

As I walked through Red Square in Moscow, Russia, I was feeling rather foreign and alone. Fascinated by the awesomeness of the walled Kremlin, I thought of the violent history that had taken place there. Then, my attention was caught by a sparrow perched on the branch of a lilac tree, on the grounds of nearby St. Basil's Cathedral. It was happily chirping away, unabashedly confident that it was just as important as the passersby or any of the great historical buildings.

The thought of our Heavenly Father watching over that little sparrow in Red Square, encouraged me. I felt at peace and loved in a foreign land. As I watched the faces of the Russian people, who had been oppressed for so long, I prayed that they, too, would come to know the Giver of that same peace.

Consider
The lilies of the field, who blossom in brief—
We are like they;
Like them we fade away,
As does a leaf.

Consider
The sparrows of the air, of small account:
Our God doth view
Whether they fall or mount—
He guards us, too.

Consider
The lilies, that do neither spin nor toil,
Yet are most fair—
What profits all His care,
And all this toil?

Consider
The birds that have no barn nor harvest weeks:
God gives them food—
Much more our Father seeks
To do us good.

CHRISTINA ROSSETTI

As a child, I would spend hours, watching as birds would build their nests in our garden. They showed such determination as they gathered twigs, moss and other materials to construct their homes. I would search the house for suitable things to help make their nests warm. A small doll would be minus a sweater, or my grandmother would find wool missing from her sewing basket as I endeavored to assist them. Strewing my finds under the tree where they were building their nests, I would then run back into the house and watch how hard they worked, marvelling at the way God had created such amazing instincts in those little creatures.

> *This little bird has had its supper, and now it is getting ready to sleep here, quite secure and content, never troubling itself what its food will be, or where its lodging on the morrow. Like David, it 'abides under the shadow of the Almighty.' It sits on its little twig content, and lets God take care.*
>
> MARTIN LUTHER

The little cares that fretted me,
I lost them yesterday,
Among the fields above the sea,
Among the winds at play,
Among the lowing of the herds,
The rustling of the trees,
Among the singing of the birds,
The humming of the bees.
The foolish fears of what might pass
I cast them all away
Among the clover-scented grass
Among the new-mown hay,
Among the rustling of the corn
Where drowsy poppies nod.
Where ill thoughts die and good are born——
Out in the fields with God!

ELIZABETH BARRETT BROWNING

Once when I was going through a dark period I prayed and
prayed, but the heavens seemed to be brass. I felt as though
God had disappeared and that I was all alone with my trial
and burden. It was a dark night for my soul. I wrote my mother
about the experience, and will never forget her reply: 'Son,
there are many times when God withdraws to test your faith.
He wants you to trust Him in the darkness. Now, Son, reach
up by faith in the fog and you will find that His hand will be
there.' In tears I knelt by my bed and experienced an overwhelm-
ing sense of God's presence. Whether or not we sense and feel
the presence of the Holy Spirit or one of the holy angels, by
faith we are certain God will never leave us nor forsake us.

BILLY GRAHAM

The nightly news had reported that Spokane airport was experiencing icy conditions. The next morning I kept remembering that, as my husband and I drove eighty miles through a blizzard to get there. Cars had gone off the road and men with snow ploughs were bravely fighting the blinding storm.

I half hoped the airport would be closed and we would have to spend the night in a warm motel, but when we finally reached there, all systems were "go." Through the lounge windows, I could see the very small twin engine plane that would take us to a connecting flight in Seattle. I was not reassured.

After several delays, while the ground crew inspected and walked around the plane looking for any evidence of ice by twirling each of the propellers, I found myself strapped in and anxiously looking out of the window. Having been through earthquakes, an air crash, air raids and storms at sea, I began remembering words that might comfort me. "God never changes." "Somewhere the sun is always shining." But I still kept watching the snow, as it buffeted against the little craft and asked for His peace.

The engines started and we raced down the runway into what looked like oblivion. "Well, Lord," I thought, "this might be the day when I come to the end of my earthly life... I'm

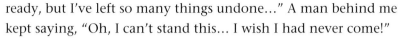

ready, but I've left so many things undone..." A man behind me kept saying, "Oh, I can't stand this... I wish I had never come!"

The plane shuddered, as we rose into leaden skies, filled with the never-ending snow. We were thrown around like tenpins, as the winds buffeted the plane.

Then came the pilot's voice, calm and reassuring. "Hang in there, I'll get you through this in a few minutes..." Up through the gray clouds, with visibility at zero, climbed the gallant small plane. For several minutes it felt as if we would never see light again and then... the sun was shining, the skies were a brilliant blue, and instead of the turmoil of a storm, there was peace.

I looked out the small window and soaked in the beauty of it all. I knew that down below all was chaos. I wanted to remember that magnificent scene.

It reminded me of how often our lives are filled with discouragement, and what seems like no way out, but if we look up through the heartaches, we come closer to Jesus Christ. His words, even as the pilot's had comforted me, will reassure and give us the strength to rise above our own personal storms.

> *I believe in the sun, even when it is not shining—*
> *I believe in Love, even when I feel it not—*
> *I believe in God, even when He is silent.*
> THE WALLS OF A CELLAR IN COLOGNE, GERMANY

> *Give me faith, Lord, and let me help others to find it.*
> LEO TOLSTOY

*M*any years ago there was an old man who had come to Washington, D.C. on a vital mission. A young boy found him sitting by a wall which surrounded the White House. He saw that tears were rolling down the old man's cheeks, so he went over and asked him what was the matter.

"Oh, young man, my son is in the Army. He's been arrested for desertion and condemned to death. I've tried to get in to see President Lincoln, but the guards will not allow me in."

"I can take you to the President," said the boy.

"You can?" The old man looked at the boy in astonishment.

"Yes, sir, he's my father. He lets me come in anytime."

Abraham Lincoln received the distraught father and listened to his plea. His son was granted a pardon and the old man went away rejoicing.

When we come to God, in faith, asking for a pardon for our sins, He grants our petition because of His Son, Jesus Christ. We always have access to Him wherever we are.

*A*t certain times in my life, I have felt angry—angry at God. I have prayed earnestly for someone to be healed of sorrow or suffering without any sense of positive change. Concerns for my loved ones have overwhelmed me and in my cries to God, there was a silence that brought me to tears. C.S. Lewis in "A Grief Observed," aptly describes our sense of loss in a situation like this: "A door slammed in your face, and a sound of bolting and double bolting on the inside. After that silence."

Although unanswered prayers can leave us wondering if God truly cares, I've found that my anger always subsides when I think of Jesus and ask God's forgiveness for my outbursts. In the mystery of the Trinity, it is the "Man of Sorrows" we can relate to most easily. After all, how could my anger last when I pause to think of His great sacrifice for me—for all of us. His Love was unconditional as He hung upon the Cross and prayed, "Father, forgive them, for they know not what they do." Even He experienced the terrible feelings of isolation and abandonment, when He cried out, "Why hast thou forsaken me?"

In the quietness of my relationship with Him, even though I cannot understand why some prayers are not answered the way I desire and others are, I can, by faith in Him believe that He is guiding my life and the lives of those I love. Then comes the peace that passes all understanding.

With eager heart and will on fire,
I fought to win my great desire.
"Peace shall be mine," I said, but life
Grew bitter in the weary strife.
My soul was tired, and my pride
Was wounded deep: to Heaven I cried,
"God grant me peace or I must die;"
The dumb stars glittered no reply.
Broken at last, I bowed my head,
Forgetting all myself, and said,
"Whatever comes, His will be done;"
And in that moment peace was won.

HENRY VAN DYKE

Let Thy will be mine, and let my will always
        follow Thine,
        and agree perfectly therewith. . .
Grant that I may rest in Thee above all
        things that can be desired,
        and that my heart may be at peace in Thee.
Thou art the true peace of the heart, Thou
        art its only rest;
        out of Thee all things are irksome and restless.
In this very peace which is in Thee,
        the one Supreme Eternal Good,
        I will sleep and take my rest.

THOMAS a KEMPIS

Wings of Comfort

He shall cover you with His feathers,
And under His wings you shall take refuge;
His truth shall be your shield and buckler.

PSALMS 91: 4

*T*he singularly beautiful symbol for the Holy Spirit is the dove, the gentlest of birds. Just to look at it, brings comfort and a feeling of tranquillity. In the stained glass windows of cathedrals and churches throughout the world, its image reminds us of God's Spirit, forever the refuge of those who love Him.

In Westminister Abbey, several years ago, at a time when a loved one was going through extreme difficulties, I heard the great choir singing, "O, for the wings, for the wings of a dove." The glorious sound of the organ and the ethereal voices of the young choristers filled my being and I found it hard to control my emotions. As I sat and listened, I could feel God's presence and my prayers took wing and soared up to the very heights of heaven. I found comfort in the beauty of those words of David's:

"So I said, Oh, that I had wings like a dove!
I would fly away and be at rest."

PSALMS 55:6

That day I did find rest, knowing that my loved one was in God's hands and that He would indeed, answer my heartfelt prayers. Several years have passed since I attended that service and I continue to see the wonder of His touch in the life of the one I prayed for so earnestly.

Breathe, O breathe Thy loving Spirit
Into every troubled breast!
Let us all in Thee inherit,
Let us find the promised rest.

CHARLES WESLEY

The Psalms have been a lifeline for me. In times of joy, I have praised God with David's melodious words, worshiped Him with his lyrical poetry. In times of tragedy and bereavement, I have found consolation and hope. My soul finds in them a comforting, yet sometimes challenging place.

In the Psalter it states, "The Psalms are the many-toned voice of prayer in the widest sense, as the soul's address to God in confession, petition, intercession, meditation, thanksgiving and praise, both in public and private."

One of the most comforting Psalms is the 91st. It tells of God's compassionate love towards us. It is filled with promises of a safe refuge—a fortress for our defense.

When we dwell beneath His protective wings, He provides us with His care, shielding us from our enemies, even illness. We need not be afraid of the darkness of this world, for He will summon His angels to keep us safe. What a comforting promise this is!

As we know and love God through Jesus Christ, our lives are protected in the shadow of His love, and in the last verse of Psalm 91, we are assured of deliverance—not only in this life, but for eternity.

With long life I will satisfy him,
and show him My salvation.

PSALMS 91:16

Prayer is the wing wherewith the soul flies
to heaven, and meditation the eye wherewith
we see God.

SAINT AMBROSE

More things are wrought by prayer
Than this world dreams of.
Wherefore, let thy voice
Rise like a fountain for me night and day.
For what are men better than sheep or goats
That nourish a blind life within the brain,
If knowing God, they lift not hands of prayer
Both for themselves and those who call them
friend?
For so the whole round earth is every way
Bound by gold chains about the feet of God.

ALFRED, LORD TENNYSON

Be not forgetful of prayer.
Every time you pray, if your prayer is sincere,
there will be new feeling and new meaning in it,
which will give you fresh courage…

FEDOR DOSTOEVSKI

*H*ow many times I have needed courage—courage to face a situation from which I would rather have run: Seeing a loved one leaving on a plane, knowing it would mean months of separation, yet pretending I was fine; waiting in the impersonal surroundings of a hospital while my husband or child was being operated on and wanting only to shout, "Stop, don't do it!" but knowing it had to be; or groping for courage to get out of my car and have tests that might prove that I, too, needed major surgery.

How do we cope? How do we face the crises in our own lives?

To say I can face stress on my own would be untrue. Without the presence and the power of God, I would crumble under the strain. It is the assurance of His presence that gives me the courage to go on. Through prayer I come to Him and pour out all my needs and in the quiet of my room, or in the turmoil of this world, He gives me the necessary strength.

> *And I will pray the Father, and He will give you*
> *another Helper, that He may abide with you forever.*
>   JOHN 14:16

*O*nce while my husband was undergoing cancer surgery, the power of God's Holy Spirit comforted us. I waited, prayerfully, as the twelve and a half hour operation was being performed, and had constant assurance that I was not alone. God's presence filled that lonely room. When I felt that I was beginning to break from sheer tiredness, I quietly repeated to myself Psalms 42:11 from the Living Bible:

But O my soul, don't be discouraged. Don't be upset.
Expect God to act! For I know that I shall again have plenty
of reason to praise him for all that he will do. He is my
help! He is my God!

PSALMS 42:11

There was plenty of reason to praise Him, for Bill came through the operation amazingly well. The prayers of our family and friends were answered and we were humbled by his complete healing.

I have used this verse in many situations. Sometimes when I have recited it aloud, I have felt as if I could not even manage to get to the end, but there comes a strength that is not my own and I know that His Spirit, the Comforter, is with me, whatever the outcome.

And so I find it well to come
For deeper rest to this still room;
For here the habit of the soul
Feels less the outer world's control
And from the silence, multiplied
By these still forms on every side,
The world that time and sense has known
Falls off and leaves us God alone.

JOHN GREENLEAF WHITTIER

I will lift up my eyes to the hills—
From whence comes my help?
My help comes from the Lord,
Who made heaven and earth.
He will not allow your foot to be moved:
He who keeps you will not slumber.
Behold, He who keeps Israel
Shall neither slumber nor sleep.
The Lord is your keeper;
The Lord is your shade at your right hand.
The sun shall not strike you by day,
Nor the moon by night.
The Lord shall preserve you from all evil;
He shall preserve your soul.
The Lord shall preserve your going out
and your coming in
From this time forth, and even forevermore.

PSALMS 121

*T*he beauty of nature, whether observed firsthand, in a painting, or described in a poem, can bring us tranquillity. Such poetry was written by William Wordsworth, who lived in the beautiful Lake Country of England. The magnificent countryside served as inspiration for many of his works. "I wandered lonely as a cloud...", his hauntingly exquisite poem about daffodils, was written from a memory of discovering a whole bank of these sun-filled flowers.

On a visit to the French Riviera, he was inspired to write a sonnet to his ten-year-old daughter Carolyn. As they walked along the beach at sunset, he composed these serene words:

It is a beauteous evening, calm and free;
The holy time is quiet as a nun
Breathless with adoration; the broad sun
Is sinking down in its tranquillity;
The gentleness of heaven broods o'er the sea;
Listen! the mighty Being is awake,
And doth with his eternal motion make
A sound like thunder—everlastingly.
Dear child! dear girl! that walkest with me here,
If thou appear untouched by solemn thought,
Thy nature is not therefore less divine:
Thou liest in Abraham's bosom all the year,
And worship'st at the Temple's inner shrine,
God being with thee when we know it not.

WILLIAM WORDSWORTH

When I was a young child, shortly after the death of my mother, my father took me on vacation. We stayed at a small hotel overlooking a harbor. One night a storm was brewing out to sea and I watched the black clouds rolling closer toward the shore. It began to rain as I got ready for bed. My father was downstairs talking to some of the other guests, when a huge flash of lightning, followed by a deafening clap of thunder, made the lights go out. Frightened, I began to cry, wondering where my father was.

Then I heard my father's voice calling to me as he came up the stairs. "Don't be afraid, Joan. I'm here. Everything is all right."

The sound of his reassuring voice took away all my fears, and his presence in the room enabled me to sleep peacefully, knowing he would protect me.

Dear Lord and Father of mankind!
Forgive our foolish ways!
Reclothe us in our rightful mind,
In purer lives Thy service find,
In deeper reverence, praise. . . .
Drop Thy still dews of quietness,
Till all our strivings cease;
Take from our souls the strain and stress,
And let our ordered lives confess
The beauty of Thy peace.

JOHN GREENLEAF WHITTIER

I first read these words on a day when difficult problems were overwhelming me. The noise of the traffic in London, England, caused me to enter a church to find peace. Only two other people were in the great sanctuary, their heads bowed in prayer.

I slipped quietly into one of the pews and sat there feeling utterly shattered from the strain of another frustratingly hurtful day. I could not bring my thoughts together to even pray. Seeing a hymnal, I began to idly turn the pages and found hymns that I had learned as a child. Their familiarity comforted me, yet still, I found no peace. Then I read Whittier's words and they seemed to leap out at me:

"Drop Thy still dews of quietness,
Till all our strivings cease..."

Reflecting on these words, I found I was able to pray, and I asked our Lord to take away the stress that kept me from communing with Him. In a few quiet moments, I regained my composure. All my concerns were stripped away and I found the comfort of His wings. I asked for His will to be done in my life

and forgiveness for so often going ahead of Him. I found the
serenity and strength that I needed to face the day. Leaving the
church, I walked down the same noisy streets, but no longer
alone. His presence was with me.

I do not know what the future holds
    Of joy or pain
    Of loss or gain
Along life's untrod way;
    But I believe
    I can receive
God's promised guidance day by day;
    So I securely travel on.
And if at times, the journey leads
    Through waters deep,
    Or mountains steep,
I know this unseen Friend,
    His love revealing,
    His presence healing,
Walks with me to the journey's end;
    So I securely travel on.

AUTHOR UNKNOWN

*A*leksandr Solzhenitsyn, the brilliant Russian writer, knew what it was to be persecuted. His harsh prison sentence in the Gulag would have broken many a man, but his was an iron will that withstood the terror and deprivation. After years of hardship in Communist Russia, he writes this testimony to his faith:

> *How easy for me to live with You, O Lord!*
> *How easy for me to believe in You!*
> *When my mind parts in bewilderment or falters,*
> *when the most intelligent people see no further*
> *than this day's end and do not know what must be done*
> *tomorrow,*
> *You grant me the serene certitude that You exist*
> *and that You will take care that not all*
> *the paths of good be closed,*
>
> *Atop the ridge of earthly fame,*
> *I look back in wonder at*
> *the path which I alone could never have found,*
> *a wondrous path through despair to the point*
> *from which I, too, could transmit to mankind*
> *a reflection of Your rays.*
> *And as much as I must still reflect*
> *You will give me.*
> *But as much as I cannot take up*
> *You will have already assigned to others.*
> ALEKSANDR SOLZHENITSYN

*T*he faith of the woman in Mark 5:25-32, who had been ill for twelve years, is a courageous example, for she believed that if only she could touch Jesus she would be healed. She had heard of this Man who could raise people from the dead, and heal lepers. Surely He could heal her! Each day she hoped that her sickness would be conquered. Gradually, her strength ebbed away and, perhaps,even her faith began to falter. Then came the news that He was to pass by and summoning any strength she had, she went out into the crowd that waited for Him.

The press of the people around her must have caused her to almost faint, yet she persisted in pushing herself closer and closer. All she wanted was to touch His robe, believing that she would be healed. Weak and faint from the insufferable heat of the sun, she waited for Jesus.

At last she saw Him, surrounded by His disciples, and she desperately pushed forward to be close enough to kneel and touch the hem of His garment.

Instantly, Jesus knew that someone had touched Him in a special way, and He asked His disciples, "Who touched me?" Astounded, they answered, "You see the crowds around you and you ask, who touched you?" It was impossible for them to tell, yet Jesus knew and turned to look at that frail woman. As she saw His compassionate eyes upon her, she became afraid, even though she knew something incredible had happened to her. She knelt down before Him and told Him the truth about herself.

Think of the joy that must have come over her, as Jesus said, "Daughter, your faith has made you well. Go in peace and be healed of your affliction."

Those words apply to us today. When we come to Jesus in absolute faith and trust, pouring out all our needs, our hurts, and our longings, He heals our troubled minds of whatever is plaguing us. When we are honest in our communion with Him, then we are never alone in our sorrows. We are never just "someone in the crowd" to our Lord.

When Jesus healed the man blind from birth
He let him grope his way, still blind,
to wash in the pool—and then the light broke.
We don't need to know what we're groping
toward—or why. It is enough that we have
Christ's direction. The light will break
in God's own time.

AUTHOR UNKNOWN

Sometimes a light surprises
The Christian while he sings;
It is the Lord who rises
With healing in his wings.
When comforts are declining
He grants the soul again
A season of clear shining,
To cheer it after rain.

WILLIAM COWPER

*W*ith a heart cry to God, I have thanked Him that He is with me and knows the extent to which this frame can be bent, but not broken. I often need His resiliency in my life, so that the branches of my mind will not snap, when times come that make life difficult to bear.

Understanding the Psalms, helps us see we no longer need to feel guilty for the impassioned feelings that sometimes sweep over us. When David wrote those masterpieces, he created a place of refuge for us to follow. Anyone suffering mental anguish could look to them and find comfort. He knew the deepest valleys and was not afraid to tell God the truth about himself.

If we were always on a mountaintop, we would miss what God would teach us in the valleys—that even on days when we feel He is unreachable, He is there. It is at this time we have to rely completely on faith and say, "Lord, I do not feel Your presence with me, but I know that You are there and this wilderness is only temporary in my life."

> *Peace I leave with you, My peace I give to you;*
> *not as the world gives, do I give to you.*
> *Let not your heart be troubled, neither let it be*
> *afraid.*

JOHN 14:27

*I*n the midst of tragedy, Horatio Gates Spafford wrote the consoling hymn, "It Is Well With My Soul." It was at a time in his life when he had suffered unbearable loss. Spafford's home was destroyed in the Great Chicago fire, but fortunately, his family escaped unhurt. They were thankful that they had been spared and could build another home. At the time, Spafford realized that possessions meant nothing—his family, everything. He did not know then, that in only a few weeks, a greater tragedy would occur.

It was decided that Spafford's wife and four daughters should visit France. The children talked excitedly to him, as they stood on the dock, waiting to see their ship sail. Kissing them good-bye, he hugged each one and looked forward to the day when they would all be together again.

During the crossing, their ship, the "Ville du Havre", was rammed by another vessel. Within two hours, two hundred and twenty-six people were drowned. Spafford's wife was rescued, but his four daughters were lost.

On learning the tragic news, Spafford left for Europe to join his grief-stricken wife. One night at sea, in December 1873, the captain of his ship showed him the spot where the tragedy had occurred. Devastated, Spafford returned to his cabin and spent a night in prayer, pouring out his grief to the Lord. As he prayed, he felt the comfort of Christ's love, and out of the despair of this dark experience he wrote a hymn of triumphant peace and acceptance of the will of God:

When peace like a river attendeth my way
When sorrows like sea billows roll;
Whatever my lot, Thou hast taught me to say,
It is well, it is well with my soul.

We all live uncertain lives, never knowing when tragedy might strike: but we can know that whatever happens, there will be the certainty of Jesus Christ's presence. What a difference it makes to our peace of mind. When our fears take over,we have to center our thoughts on Jesus—asking Him to take away the agonizing doubts, the emotions that we find so hard to control. In the comforting knowledge that He is with us, we are able to find that peace that only He can give.

God, make me brave for life: oh, braver than this.
Let me straighten after pain,
as a tree straightens after the rain,
Shining and lovely again.

HORATIO GATES SPAFFORD

Wings of Hope

They that wait upon the Lord
shall renew their strength;
they shall mount up with wings like eagles...

ISAIAH 40: 31

*W*hat incredible words! To think that those who love the Lord receive spiritual wings! He gives us the capacity to soar above the world's difficulties and see them for what they are. He brings hope for all our tomorrows.

The illustration of the eagle is one of strength. His great wing span enables him to fly high above the earth and with keenness of sight, he is able to observe his prey at great distances. It is no wonder that armies and countries have chosen this bird for their standards, a symbol of royal power. In 1782, by an Act of Congress, the eagle became the emblem for the United States of America.

A mother eagle has great affection for her young and is very solicitous of their well-being. She hovers over their nest, stirring them up when they would sooner be sleeping. Her fluttering shows them how to fly and when they are old enough she takes them on her wings, until they learn to fly by themselves.

When it is time for her offspring to leave the nest, she destroys it, a seemingly radical action. Yet the young eaglets soon realize they must learn to fly on their own. They can no longer cling to the security of their familiar home. The mother eagle knows it is best for their future, for they must now fend for themselves.

*S*ometimes in our lives, it seems God allows what we have held dear to be destroyed. He stirs our nest and we are bewildered by His actions. Our security is threatened and we feel abandoned. But He will not leave us without hope.

May we take heart and know that He is a loving Father and what may seem hard to us is really His way of teaching us to "fly." We can use our spiritual wings to see His perspective and not our own. I believe He teaches us to hold lightly the things in our lives that are transitory.

Our wings of hope help us to transcend the valleys and alight on the mountain top like the eagle, and from that viewpoint we are able to have a clearer vision of the Lord's plan for our life.

The wing life is characterized by comprehensiveness.
High soaring gives wide seeing.

DR. JOWETT

Hope is an 'inseparable companion' of both faith and love. Hope is nothing else than the expectation of those things which faith has believed to have been promised by God.

JOHN KNOX

Jesus said to him, If you can believe,
all things are possible to him that believes.
Immediately the father of the child cried
out and said with tears,"Lord, I believe;
help my unbelief!"

MARK 9:23,24

*H*ow reassuring these words are to those of us who suffer doubts! The father of the sick child was desperate to see his son healed, yet pounding in his agonized mind were questions that led him to believe that perhaps Jesus would not heal him.

As we read these words we are consoled by the fact that Jesus knew there were questions—fears—this man was experiencing. Was it possible for his child to be healed? Could Jesus really perform a miracle? Then the father cries out, "Lord, I believe; help my unbelief!" Here is a crucial moment, one with which we may identify.

When I first encountered this verse, I was thankful that the besieged father had been so truthful concerning his unbelief. Here was an example of our Lord's compassion, for when this man cried out in truth to Him, Jesus healed his son. However, would He not have been a compassionate Christ if the child had died?

In a *New York Times* article concerning healing, it was stated that sometimes God heals through our prayers and sometimes He answers by allowing those who are so ill to go to be with Him. I believe if we only knew all that awaits us in heaven, we would say with conviction, "God does not make mistakes!"

He does not make mistakes, even though I have questioned why He allows those who have so much to give this world to die. A six-year-old cousin of mine died of leukemia when I was young.

He was a beautiful, fun-loving child who brought nothing but joy to those who loved him. When he died, our world was shattered. His parents never really got over their heartache. My aunt, his mother, turned to our Lord for comfort and gradually

came to accept his death; believing it was not the end, but the beginning of a life spent forever with his Savior. She lives with the belief that one day she will see her son again.

This is the hope that each one of us who have suffered bereavement can embrace, for Jesus Christ has conquered the finality of death; and as we look to Him, His love will continually reach down into our sorrowing hearts:

Can I see another's woe,
And not be in sorrow too?
Can I see another's grief
And not seek for kind relief?

Can I see a falling tear,
And not feel my sorrow's share?

He doth give his joy to all;
He becomes an infant small;
He becomes a man of woe;
He doth feel the sorrow, too.

Think not thou canst sigh a sigh
And thy maker is not by;
Think not thou canst weep a tear
And thy maker is not near.

Oh! he gives to us his joy
That our grief he may destroy…

WILLIAM BLAKE

Three times Roy and I have felt the painful
laceration of death as we stood, crushed,
by the graveside of our children. To call these 'hard
times' seems the understatement of the century.
These were intensely human moments for me.
The deep hurt seared through my body
like a rampaging forest fire in our California mountains.
But even in the midst of my pain,
I knew somehow that God stood near in my lonely walk
'through the valley of the shadow of death' and that his
'goodness and mercy' were with me
and would stay with me forever.

DALE EVANS ROGERS

Yea, though I walk
through the valley of the shadow of death
I will fear no evil,
for You are with me;
Your rod and Your staff,
they comfort me.

PSALMS 23

For God so loved the world that He gave
His only begotten Son, that whosoever
believes in Him should not perish,
but have everlasting life.

JOHN 3:16

The knocking on the door and Mary Magdalene's urgent voice awakened the disciples out of their despair, when she told them that she had seen the Lord—that He had risen as He said He would! What joy, excitement, and even doubt, must have crowded their minds as they ran back to the garden where the tomb was and saw with their own eyes that the stone had been rolled away and that the tomb was empty!

No gravestone would ever be inscribed, HERE LIES JESUS CHRIST, for He is alive!

> *He rose!*
> *And with Him hope arose, and life and light.*
> *Men said, "Not Christ but Death died yesternight."*
> *And joy and truth and all things virtuous*
> *Rose, when He rose.*
>
> AUTHOR UNKNOWN

During the reign of Queen Victoria, a young boy was walking down a street in London, when he noticed a large painting of the Crucifixion displayed in a shop window. He stopped and looked at it for a long time, lost in thought. A man was walking by and seeing the child so enraptured by the painting, he stopped, too.

After a moment or so, the young boy looked up at him and said, "That's Jesus on the Cross, and those soldiers, they're the ones that killed Him."

"Who told you that?" the man asked.

"I learned it in Sunday School, sir."

The man said nothing, then began to walk away, deep in

thought. He had gone only a few steps, when the young boy ran after him.

"I forgot to tell you, Sir, the most important part—that He rose again!"

The man looked down at him and smiled. "Thank you for telling me that, young man," and went on his way.

The victorious message of Easter was almost forgotten. Because Jesus rose again, He triumphed over death and we can now be assured of eternal life with Him. This glorious knowledge brings joy to each of our lives; and in the words of Peter Marshall, "Let us never live another day as if He were dead!"

> *All shall be well,*
> *and all shall be well*
> *and all manner of thing*
> *shall be well.*
>
> JULIAN OF NORWICH

> *Here we have no continuing city,*
> *but we seek one to come.*
>
> HEBREWS 13:14

I have lived in many houses. As a child, I had at least ten different homes. My mother's death, when I was four, and World War II contributed to making my childhood a transient one. Since then, there have been many moves, some pleasant—others best forgotten! Always, I dreamed of the perfect place that one day would be my home.

Finally, after being married for over fifteen years and moving twenty-one times, my husband Bill and I bought our first house.

It was exciting moving in, decorating and making a real home. "I'll never want to move again," I thought, and happily went about the task of homemaking. Seeing the children grow and thrive meant so much to my husband and me. Yet, there was still something missing. Perhaps we needed a larger house? One more bedroom? A larger garden? I was forgetting that wherever we moved, we were still pilgrims, looking for that "continuing city."

Each of our lives is a pilgrimage. When we know that heaven is our home, then there is a restlessness, a longing. Sometimes the bridge between this world and our eternal home will bring heartache and suffering. Sometimes, thoughts of the unknown may make us fearful.

What hope we have because of Jesus Christ! It is comforting to know that we will not be alone, for the shelter of His wings will gently guide us. He will be our "inseparable companion", and when we arrive we shall see our Savior face-to-face!

We only see a little of the ocean,
A few miles distance from the rocky shore;
But oh! out there beyond—beyond the eyes' horizon
There's more—there's more.
We only see a little of God's loving,
A few rich treasures from His mighty store;
But oh! out there beyond—beyond our life's horizon
There's more—there's more.

AUTHOR UNKNOWN

No coward soul is mine,
No trembler in the world's storm-troubled sphere:
I see Heaven's glories shine,
And faith shines equal, arming me from fear.

O God within my breast,
Almighty, ever present Deity!
Life—that in me hast rest,
As I, undying Life, have power in thee!

Though earth and moon were gone,
And suns and universes ceased to be,
And thou were left alone,
Every existence would exist in Thee.

There is not room for Death,
Nor atom that his might could render void:
Thou—Thou art Being and Breath,
And what Thou art may never be destroyed.

EMILY BRONTE

Let not your heart be troubled; you believe in God,
believe also in Me. In My Father's house are many
mansions; if it were not so, I would have told you.
I go to prepare a place for you. And if I go and
prepare a place for you, I will come again
and receive you to Myself; that where I am,
there you may be also.

JOHN 14: 1-3

*S*everal years ago, while I was living in London I received news that my grandmother was dying. Immediately, memories of childhood flooded me as I thought of the woman who had helped raise me after my mother died. Nanny, as I called her, had been so wonderful; always finding time to play and take care of a hyper-child. Now she was dying, and as I left to go to the hospital, I prayed the Lord would give me the right words to comfort her.

I remembered how she reacted in times past, when I told her how much God loved her —-a blank stare from Nanny and then silence. On one visit, I had reiterated to her about His love, and she had said, "It's too late for me, I'm too old to change." Another thought ran through my mind—Nanny was afraid of dying.

Entering the hospital, as I took the elevator, I prayed that the Lord would help me tell her all that was in my heart. A nurse told me Nanny's condition had worsened. Walking into her room, I saw her lying there, small and helpless in a sterile hospital bed. The room, devoid of any decoration, made her seem even more the poignant focus of attention.

"Nanny," I whispered. She opened her eyes and there was a flicker of recognition. I took her hand in mine.

I remembered, as I looked at that work-worn hand, how many times I had held it as we had gone on adventures together. I desperately wanted to convey to her my thanks and love for all that she had ever done for me. The nurse had said it would not be long before the end.

I began to recall for her the happy days we spent together, telling her how much I loved her and how grateful I was for all she did for me.

"Nanny, do you know that Jesus loves you?"

There was a slight pause and then she said, very softly, "Yes."

"And do you know He has a place waiting for you that is far more beautiful than anything you have ever seen?"

Her face began to light up as she said, "Yes, I know!"

Her limp hand, which I was still holding, pressed mine in silent affirmation. I looked at her face and Nanny never looked more beautiful to me, for now there was an expression of joy and hope in her eyes.

I leaned over and kissed her, telling her again how much I loved her and that one day we would all be together again. She smiled and nodded.

As the time came for me to leave, I said, "Good-bye," and she waved to me. Her dear face relayed the peace she had found. That is my last memory of her.

She died a few hours later. I learned that after I left, Nanny said to her nurse, "I'm not afraid to die any more," and then slipped into a coma from which she never awakened.

How thankful I was that Nanny was with Jesus, suffering no more pain and in a place that was far more beautiful than she had ever known.

The tears I shed were human ones, the natural grief of losing a loved one, but they were also tears of gratitude that she was with the Lord—and that we are never too old to find Him.

Afraid? Of what?
To feel the spirit's glad release?
To pass from pain to perfect peace?
The strife and strains of life to cease?
Afraid—of that?

Afraid? Of what?
Afraid to see the Savior's face?
To hear His welcome, and to trace
The glory gleam from wounds of grace?
Afraid—of that?

E. H. HAMILTON

A dear friend of mine, the widow of Eric Liddell, the Scottish runner, whose life became known to millions through the movie, "Chariots of Fire," was a woman of great hope. Though her beloved husband died in a Japanese concentration camp during World War II, Florence Liddell kept those around her buoyed with her belief in Jesus Christ. In faith, she believed that one day she would be reunited with Eric.

To be with Florence Liddell, even when she was suffering great physical problems, made people feel better. She had a smile that could disarm anyone, and a love for people that could quickly dispel feelings of hopelessness.

When Florence knew she would soon go to be with her Lord, she selected a poem of hope to be read at her funeral. She wanted people to be filled with confidence, not sorrow.

Sunset and evening star,
And one clear call for me!
And may there be no moaning at the bar,
When I put out to sea.
Twilight and evening bell
And after that the dark!
And may there be no sadness of farewell,
When I embark.
For tho' from out our bourne of Time and Place
The flood may bear me far,
I hope to see my Pilot face to face
When I have crost the bar.

ALFRED, LORD TENNYSON

Think of stepping on shore and finding it Heaven!
Of taking hold of a hand and finding it God's!
Of breathing a new air and finding it celestial air!
Of feeling invigorated and finding it immortality!
Of passing from storm and stress to a perfect calm!
Of waking and finding it Home!

AUTHOR UNKNOWN

And now, Lord, what do I wait for?
My hope is in You.

PSALMS 39:7

ACKNOWLEDGMENTS

The editor and publisher have made every effort to trace the ownership of all copyrighted material and secure permission from copyright holders of such material. In the event of any question arising to the use of any material, the publisher and editor, while expressing regret for inadvertent error, will be pleased to make any necessary corrections in future printings.

Lines from "Prayers for Fellow Prisoners" are excerpted with permission of Macmillan Publishing Company from LETTERS AND PAPERS FROM PRISON, Revised ED., by Dietrich Bonhoeffer Copyright © 1953, 1967 by SCM Press Ltd.

Excerpts from ANGELS by Dr. Billy Graham Copyright © 1975 Word, Inc., Dallas, Texas. Used with permission.

Excerpts from GOD IN THE HARD TIMES, Dale Evans Rogers Copyright © 1977 Word, Inc., Dallas, Texas. Used with permission.

"Dear God, Let Me Soar" from SITTING BY MY LAUGHING FIRE Copyright © 1977 Ruth Bell Graham. Used with permission.

Excerpts from TRAILS, TEARS AND TRIUMPHS Copyright © Catherine Jackson. Published by Fleming H. Revell, a division of Baker Book House Company.

THE CHRISTIAN'S SECRET OF A HAPPY LIFE Copyright © 1979 Catherine Jackson. Excerpt by Hannah Whitall Smith (paraphrased by Catherine Jackson) published by Fleming H. Revell, a division of Baker Book House Company.

"Prayer" by Aleksandr Solzhenitsyn from SOLZHENITSYN Copyright © 1974 Farrar, Strauss and Giroux, Inc. English translation.

Cover/book design and production to disk-ready
by Markus Frey, Stamford, CT.
Edited by Karen Artl
Typset in Stone Serif/Stone Serif italic 10/15pt
Printed on Warren Patina Matte